FLYING SAUCER INTELLIGENCES SPEAK

Ted Owens

SAUCERIAN PUBLISHER

ISBN:9781736731468

© 2021, Saucerian Publisher

Al rights reserved. No part of this publication maybe reproduced, translate, store in a retrieval system, or transmitted in any form or by any means, electronic, mechanical, photocopying, recording or otherwise, without prior written permision from the publisher.

Prologue

It is generally a good idea to return to the classics in any genre. This also goes for UFO literature. Rereading a book after ten or twenty years is a rewarding experience. You will discover new data and ideas you didn´t notice before. The reason, of course, is that you are, in many ways, not the same person reading the book the second or third time. Hopefully you have advanced in knowledge, experience, intellectual and spiritual discernment. A good starting point is to reread the UFO classics in order to understand the deeper mystery involved in what happened during that era.

1947 is considered by most historians of the United States as the year when the Cold War begun with the implementation of the "Truman Doctrine" to contain the propagation of world Communism, which give rise to the anti-communist hysteria of the following years. Also, 1947 was the year when the first UFO sightings were reported in the summer.

TED OWENS: (1920-1987) was born in Indiana, the USA in February 1920. He had a high I.Q. and was a member of Mensa, a well-known organization of individuals with high mental test scores. He claimed to have macro-psychokinetic (PK) powers such as controlling the weather on a large scale, directing lightning strikes, and to cause or predict accidents. He claimed to be in close contact with "Space Intelligences" who were the cause of these events. These same beings had operated on his brain to allow it to communicate directly with them.

Unlike other contactees, Owens does not claim to have taken a ride on a saucer but uses his brain as a radio set for telepathic messages to pass on to anyone interested. According to Owens, the ultimate purpose of space intelligences was for him to act as an ambassador for them to world governments.

At the official level, the phenomenon of Ted Owens has never been studied. For scientists, he is nothing more than a charlatan, a fraudster, crackpot or a mentally unhealthy person.

This small pamphlet describes the experiences of Ted Owens over some time during which he claims to have been in contact with Intelligence from Flying Saucers. Ted Owens was a prominent radio personality, making many predictions that came true as predicted. Whatever became of the SIs (Space Intelligences) that Owens claims to have been in contact? Answer: unknown. But, he knew. This edition is an authentic reproduction of the original 1968 publication printed text in shades of gray. **IMPORTANT.** Although we have attempted to maintain text integrity accurately, the present reproduction has missing and blurred pages, poor pictures from the original scanned copy. Because this material is culturally important, we have made it available as part of our commitment to protect, preserve and promote knowledge in the world.

                                                          Editor
                                                          Saucerian Publisher, 2021

FOREWORD FOR THE SECOND EDITION

Ted Owens is a controversial figure in the UFO field. He claims to have first been contacted by the SIs (Space Intelligences) in 1965. Otto Binder, in his August, 1970, SAGA article states that Owens "is not a wild-eyed "contactee". He has never met an SI face to face nor has he traveled in their ships."

Owens certainly has a lot of credentials, more than any other person before him who claimed contact with extraterrestrials. Owens is a member of Mensa, a select organization whose members must have an I.Q. of 148 or more (only two percent of all humans would qualify for membership). Owens has a recorded I.Q. of 150 which is above genius.

Owens claims some 200 predictions, all of which are documented. Owens' bestselling How to Contact Space People contains a number of sworn affidavits which back up his claims of having made predictions well in advance of the events occurring.

Owens is said to have predicted such things as the east coast blackout, UFO appearances at specific times and odd weather phenomenon. Publisher Gray Barker and writer Timothy Green Beckley claim they've received "close to 10,000 letters from people all over the world telling us that Mr. Owens had cured them of various illnesses or brought them good fortune by putting them in contact with the SIs."

Owens also has a space scroll which will be whown to the SIs. Persons can get their names placed on the scroll free of charge. The scroll "already has brought many people who have signed good luck." Owens claims the SIs will bring good luck to all signers to show their good intentions.

Recipients of Owens' red plastic disk have also achieved remarkable success, including recovering from terminal cancer, according to the PK man.

One of Ted Owens' healing acts, related by Otto Binder in the September, 1970, issue of SAGA, concerns a young Washington, D.C., girl. She received a skull fracture after being beaten by a gang. Doctors gave her only hours to live. Owens, however, went to her and the girl recovered, much to the astonishment of the doctors.

Owens send a telegram to the CIA on October 26, 1965, warning that a terrible catastrophe would occur within ten days. November 9th was the date of the big northeastern blackout.

On March 10, 1966, Ted Owens predicted that the six-year long drought in the Northwestern states would come to an end with phenomenal rainfall "in the days, weeks and months to come". In the spring of 1967 his prediction came true.

In May, 1966, LBJ was warned by Ted Owens that "a man is planning to load a small plane with high-explosives, and send the plane, kamikaze style, into the White House or the Johnson Ranch". Owens also stated he believed the man was an ex-Army flier. The following May a former Air Force pilot was arrested for threatening to crash into the White House.

Owens' most impressive prediction to my thinking was his June, 1967, prediction of three simultaneous hurricanes. In September hurricanes Beulah, Chleo and Doris filled that prediction. It should be noted that there have only been four simultaneous hurricanes since 1886.

On March 4, 1968, Owens predicted "one or more highly-placed US government officials" would be assassinated. Within three months both Robert Kennedy and Martin Luther King were shot and killed.

Finally, on July 30, 1969, Owens wrote President Nixon warning him that Cubans were planning to kidnap the president from his Key Biscayne, Florida residence. He told Nixon they would strike by water at night with fast boats. Not four weeks later a plan was uncovered that Cubans were planning to study Nixon's movements at his Florida home using scuba divers in a mission involving "Presidential security". Owens says he's 85% accurate with his predictions and admits there are some misses.

A letter published in SAUCER NEWS #74 (Spring-Summer, 1969) puzzles me. In this letter, written by Ted Owens, he states he met one of the men in black (MIB) and the MIB turned out to be one of the SIs. The man, dressed in a black suit, asked Owens if he could help Owens with his grocery bags. Owens found himself mechanically saying, "Sure". When asked if he was from India, due to his dark complexion, the MIB said yes. When they reached Owens' house the MIB gave Owens the "code phrase" which identified the MIB as an SIs. Owens crossed the street and when he looked back he found the man had vanished. Now who is right, Binder or Owens?

-Kurt Glemser

FLYING SAUCER INTELLIGENCES SPEAK

By Ted Owens

Suppose a man came to you and said that an earthquake would strike the California coast in a few days and the very next day a big earthquake on the California coast is reported in all the papers.

Then the man comes to you again and says that in two weeks time, by Halloween (1966-KG), he will try to cause a UFO to be seen and reported in the newspapers. And sure enough, on Halloween night a UFO is seen by numerous persons in Camden, N.J., headed for Philadelphia (where the man making these predictions then lived) and it is written up in the newspapers, just as the man said it would be.

The same man comes to you and says that in the days ahead an early hurricane will appear off Florida and 5 days later Hurricane Alma appears and hits Florida, the earliest hurricane in history to do so.

When Hurricane Inez is born, this man comes to you and tells you that, contrary to what the Weather Bureau says, Inez will turn right at Cuba and go to the US. It does. Then, contrary to what the Weather Bureau says, the man says the hurricane will back up and take the same track Hurricane Betsy took last year, which Inez does!

The man comes to you and says in the near future President Johnson will have a breakdown in health. In 120 days an unexpected public announcement is made that Johnson will have to have surgery.

This same fellow then says that an attack on our warships by the enemy in Vietnam is imminent. And sure enough two days later North Vietnamese torpedo boats strike with a sneak attack at our aircraft carriers.

You are told that within just days a UFO will be seen flying over Philadelphia. In six days the now famous "Fireball Over The East Coast" is written up in national magazines and in all the papers.

Then he comes to you and says that in the near future the U.S. will suffer a naval catastrophe involving aircraft carriers or submarines. Within 120 days the US aircraft carrier Criskany burns; the US nuclear sub Nautilus crashes into the US aircraft carrier Essex; altogether there are 10 U.S. catastrophes involving aircraft carriers and U.S. submarines within this period of time.

But all these miraculous predictions are nothing new to you, because this same man has been doing this same thing for years! Over 200 successful predictions all involving major events.

You would like to try and pooh-pooh all this, but you cannot, because you know the man has given you the predictions in writing ahead of the events and you know that he has also furnished various government agencies and scientists with the same information, always ahead of the event.

I am the man making these predictions. The how and what of it all is quite a long and involved account and will be put into print here for the first time.

As you might have guessed UFO intelligences were behind all of these predictions, plus over 200 others like them. What you might not have guessed is that the UFO intelligences caused all these things to happen.

How It All Started

Let's get one thing absolutely straight. I am not a "contactee" in the often thought of way. In the beginning, several years ago, I was.

It all began somehow in Fort Worth, Texas, where I had sorted out a group of three super-ESP people (one of them a doctor) who were quite advanced in clairvoyance and telepathy. I systematically used hypnotism with them, endeavoring to send their minds to seek out UFOs and establish mental contacts.

This they did with considerable success but that is another story. At that time I lived with my tiny daughter Lornie, age eight. One particular evening I was out driving along a lonely road in the Texas countryside, with my daughter in the seat next to me, just after dark. Suddenly she said, "Daddy, look. What is that?" and pointed out my driver's window to the left of our car.

I took one look and immediately pulled over to the side of the road and parked. There coming across a field towards us, about 500 feet away, was a cigar-shaped object, with vivid colours streaming from it. White, blue, red and green are the colours I remember strongly now. It seemed to be floating or gliding towards us, making no noise whatsoever. It came fairly close to our car -- I would say to within 50 feet or so -- then dipped downward and vanished completely. We had watched it for about two minutes, I believe.

Only The Beginning

After that evening, strange things began to happen. Ideas began to come to me in a flood. First these ideas helped me to write a book about healing people. Then, as the years passed, something seemed to give me intelligence about national and international events which came to pass. I thought at first that I had somehow tapped the intelligence behind Nature. I worked with this intelligence, whatever it was, and literally accomplished miracles with it, but that too is another story.

Finally I brought my family to Washington, D.C., to place all this information at the service of the United States government. But they couldn't seem to grasp what on earth it was I was doing, or had. One evening with the kids (I had my son with me then too) the intelligence came to me stronger than ever. It told me to give a man I knew in the CIA a message that it would do something at the north or south pole which would change the electromagnetic field there, and would make the newspapers. They said that when this happened it would be absolute proof of my contact with these then unknown intelligences. Weeks passed and nothing happened. Five months passed, then there it was. The South Pole UFO that parked over the two scientific expeditions, making sure it was photographed, altered the electromagnetic equipment at the basis involved. This was, of course, widely reported on in the newspapers.

After this I knew what my contacts were -- UFOs. Shortly after that happened, I received a different sort of intelligence from them, again while seated at the dining table with my two children. I will type it here exactly as it was given to me.

Intelligence From A Far Communicate

First a triangle and rectangle popped into my mind, then the letters A, B and C. I realized that had never happened before and that the UFOs must be contacting me. So I sushed the kids, grapped a pencil and paper and began making notes. The following is what came through at 10 p.m. on February 6, 1965:
"Can't come. Later we'll go find them and blot out." (Here they were talking about some satellites the government had sent up which the kids and I had been talking about just before the interruption).
"When can we meet? We know you. We are friends. Tonight is late for us. Power low. Keep open mind. We will be back with you. Your needs will be met. A study is being made of how to bring this about. Why are your people crazy? Your earth is disorganized. We would like to help organize it. We did once before, long ago in your time. People wore robes, as you call them, then, and wore beards, hair on their faces."
Question: "Can you give me an instrument, like a pencil that would do something unusual, that I could use to convince our government of your reality?"
Answer by Saucer Intelligences: "You could not use what you call a pencil, but

it is a good idea and we will send you a
tool for the purpose. You will know, repeat, know you have talked with us tonight.
We will arrange in the next few days to be
seen by your people and by that method you
will know we are making a signal for you.
Count the number of different places we
are seen and this will be the number of
days before we are able to contact you again. A magnetic condition makes it hard for
us to get through to you at all times. You
have a question?"

Question: "Yes, I need money, say
$5,000 to buy a car and go across country
to meet you. This is money (holding up a
bill I had in my pocket)."

Answer by Saucer Intelligences: "Yes,
we know money, but do not use it. (They
converse among themselves). Can you use
diamonds?"

I immediately answered that these
could be used to obtain the needed cash.
They replied that where they came from
they had lots of diamonds.

My suggestion was that they fly over
me and drop the diamonds. Their reply was
as follows: "We will think of it. If we do
we will include the tool you need to prove
to your people there must be no people-war
on earth with atomic weapons."

To this I responded that I have tried
but to no use. Their answer was a fitting:
"Yes, we did not think. Goodbye now,
friend."

So concluded their contact of February 6, 1965. One month, to the very day,
they again saw fit to communicate with me
this time with the following trade of
words:

Saucer Intelligences: "We have a plan.

Please turn that machine off. (The kids and I were listening to the radio. I switched it off.) Can't get through very good, very well. Do you have a car machine?"

Answer: "Yes, but it will not work. It's broken. That's why I need money."

Saucer Intelligences: "We are going to take care of that -- money. Do not worry about it. You will be richer than anyone in your country before long. (This is one of the things that has not come to pass. In fact if anything I have been very much without money since that time.) We want to see you, talk to you. Can we come down?"

Answer: "Yes, in my back yard. I'll let you in."

Saucer Intelligences: "Will you be alone?"

Answer: "Yes, I'll have my family upstairs."

Saucer Intelligence: "No harm will come to us?"

Answer: "No. Absolutely no. Lower your flying machine near my back door and step onto my back porch. Knock loudly on the door. I'll let you in and we can communicate. I am very pleased and anxious to meet you."

Saucer Intelligences: "Yes. We have what you need to convince your crazy people...your government...that we exist and can control your world. You can use it. It will be yours to keep."

I somehow managed to blurt out a thank you.

Saucer Intelligence: "You need a car, so that you can go far away. We will try to get you one."

Question: "My child is sick. (My baby, little Beau, had just come down with a terrible attack of red spots and high fever, diagnosed as German Measles). Also a girl, our friend, is in a hospital (this was a girl written up in the newspapers as given up as dying by the doctors, that I had been permitted, under police guard, to go visit her hospital room and use the mysterious healing method that had "come to me" in Fort Worth years before) will you heal them? (The baby got well almost instantly. The girl, previously given up for dead, because of a crushed skull began to recover and is now living in West Virginia.)"

Saucer Intelligence: "We will, indeed, heal them. Worry not. Listen carefully, no time to be lost. Your people must pay attention to you and listen to you, else we must destroy most of the earth's peoples, to begin all over again."

Question: "You mean what is happening now has happened before?"

Saucer Intelligence: "Many times."

Question: "When are you coming to see me?"

Saucer Intelligence: "Tonight we will try. Flash your light upward (my flashlight) every hour as long as you can."

Question: "Can you locate me from signals from my brain?"

Saucer Intelligence: "We can."

I then told them that I would "leave a light on so you can see". To this they replied: "No turn it off so we will not be seen by others. This is important."

Question: "Where are you from?"

Saucer Intelligence: "Some Jupiter, others other places. Even from inside this earth. Goodbye now."

Several hours later they contacted me again, that same evening. This time their message was:

Saucer Intelligence: "Do not go away, far.....Vietnam (I was trying to do so at the time, through the government). Your people will try to kill you. We need you alive. Listen carefully, there are others like us, against us, who could cause you harm. Be careful of your life, of your shell. It has taken us ages, in your time, to find a shell (means a human body) like you who can communicate with us. We do not want to lose you. But remember that you are every moment in great danger from "them" who use shellbodies. They look like and seem like real people but they are not."

Question: "Can you end the war in Vietnam and help my country, the United States, to become healthy and great again? (By "great" I didn't mean money and power but doing away with murders, gang wars, teenage violence, wholesale corruption in high and low places...a return to great moral values this country once had.)"

Saucer Intelligence: "We can and we will. But, you must not go there (Vietnam). Instead go to Hong Kong or Japan as a tourist. Go by freighter ship. We can contact you on the ship. We will defeat your enemies for you in Vietnam and bring peace. We will help your country. But your country must help you for you are our instrument. Does not your people approach certain fish to communicate with fish? (They flashed a picture of people training dolphins.) We do likewise. We go now to try to approach you. Be ready for us."

I immediately told them I would be. But they never came, and I was most disappointed. However, from the happenings at the South Pole I knew that it was not imagination. Our money got short and Lornie and Rick, my two teenagers, went off to California at the invitation of my ex-wife, who offered to see that they got into college. This was against my wishes but the kids wanted to go, so I let them. And we moved to Philadelphia. Then things began to happen fast.

Used As A Tool Of The SIs

Here the UFO intelligence went much farther then the "contactee" stage. They trained me. They gave me the tool with which to prove, without a doubt, to the U.S. government agencies, that they were real. What I am, instead of a contactee, is the only human representative of the Saucer Intelligence on this earth, able to receive intelligence from these people and transmit it to humans.

In Philadelphia the Saucer Intelligence told me to write the papers and say that I would make it storm. I did so, naming the dates, and they turned loose some fine storms (this during the height of the drought). The papers wrote this up and I was asked to appear on a big radio show in Philadelphia. The night before I was to go on radio "they" contacted me, directed me to a YMCA typewriter and had me type out a message from them to the United States. They told me to take it to the radio show and they would see that the message got to the people. I typed it, and next day went to the radio station. Since that time I have been amazing a great many people, including radio commentators, scientists and assuredly the U.S. government contacts, with predictions of national and international events which came to pass, and even more amazing when UFOs would be seen and written up in the papers. Of course the Saucer Intelligence gave me all the information. In these predictions the SIs have demonstrated their tremendous powers, including the changing of weather conditions all over the U.S., the guiding of hurricanes, the making of hurricanes and many other unbelievable things. They would tell me to write to my contacts and they would cause a California earthquake within days or weeks and sure enough, California had several big ones.

My Trip To Washington

I went to Washington, D.C., in 1965 where I had come all the way from California to present a gift they could not buy with all the gold in the U.S. mint. Now I had been writing the government for almost a year and they knew I had something tremendous because so many of the major events I had predicted in advance had come to pass.

I spent hours with George Clark of the Central Intelligence Agency. My two children, Lornie and Rick, were with me there to attest to many of the unbelievable things that had occured. Mr.Clark was a fine and intelligent man and paid the closest attention. Another time at the CIA office I was interviewed by a Mr.Dunn.

At NASA I spent hours with Mr.Eastwood, of Inventions, because much of the proof the Saucer Intelligence have been giving me involved NASA. But, they refused to take action or act on what I had told them. I was offering to place these tremendous powers in the hands of the U.S. government.

So meeting my defeat in Washington, I headed for Philadelphia. Here the Saucer Intelligence gave me a plan, which I mentioned just before, of making it storm. The <u>Philadelphia Bulletin</u> printed the story and after that I appeared on the Jack McKinney "Night Talk" radio show heard on WCAU. For four hours I was grilled by Mr. McKinney and his assistant, who attempted to find a major flaw in my work. They couldn't. They even called one of several witnesses to my predictions and had him verify what I was saying right on the program.

Several days later I was asked to appear on the Ed Harvey "Talk of Philadelphia" radio show, again on WCAU, and was asked to make it storm then, just three days away. The weather was quite clear when they called and asked. I said I would try and signalled the Saucer Intelligence and the day I appeared on the show Philadelphia was nearly ripped apart by thunder, rain and lightning!

Still, unbelievable, nothing came of all this. A full year later I was invited on the show again, this time to attest to the amazing accuracy of my predictions. But still no word from the United States government would be forthcoming.

Yet many more strange and "out of this world" experiences were about to happen which would prove the Saucer Intelligence were with me.

Another Assignment

Meanwhile the Saucer Intelligence had given me another assignment. They had found a way to get through to me and they wanted to get through to other humans. So they told me to put an advertisement in FATE Magazine re their existence and people answering the ad would be made a ring by myself. When I sent the ring to a particular person they would trace it and perhaps contact them. I, who had never made anything in my life, found myself making complicated rings in a ceramic oven!

I wasn't taught how to do this, I just suddenly knew how instantly. As far as I know no other rings have been made like this, in this way, with these materials. And it is interesting that the Saucer Intelligence had me put a certain design on the rings. Just recently, long after I began sending rings out, a UFO was observed by police officers to rise out of some woods, and the officers found a car on that spot, loaded with radio equipment and with my same design painted on the door of that car! The only deviation was that my ring design had a UFO with lightning beneath it and the car door was painted with a triangle with the lightning bolt inside it. Since I have been selling these rings one lady in Connecticut, a doctor, has had just seen UFOs recently appearing in her area so evidently the Saucer Intelligence are following up with whatever they are doing.

What The Saucer Intelligence Want

Now let's get down to business. What is this all about? Here is exactly what the Saucer Intelligence want, what I told the U.S. government long ago, what I told Jack McKinney on his radio show. They are trying to put the world in balance by cancelling out wars, hate, killing, upset weather conditions, drought, famine, etc. They can do all these things easily! But first they want a base to work from and they chose the United States. The hitch is they will not allow themselves or their apparatus to fall into the hands of humans, who are already destroying each other fast enough. They do not trust government officials, scientists, or military men. Unfortunately, since these are about the only three categories that are listened to or who have any "standing", the Saucer Intelligence have a problem on their hands. They absolutely must meet with the President and top leaders, but there is only one way this can be arranged, according to the SIs. This is the plan they sent me with to the government.

The U.S. would send me to Europe with one Special Forces man who would be my bodyguard and witness. I would be guided by the SIs to select an old deserted castle in an isolated location. I would live there for one year. Sometime during that time the Saucer Intelligence would appear to me for a face to face meeting and arrange a way to meet with the President. They would give me materials as proof. And the Special Forces man would be right with me as a witness. Why a year?

It would be difficult for agents of the United States (or some other power) to keep a trap set for one year and attempt to snare a craft.

But when I talked to the "powers that be" in Washington they would not consider this. So the Saucer Intelligence have tried an alternate plan. They don't have money, have no use for it, therefor can't furnish me with it. They want me to find a comfortable house in an isolated or semi-isolated location and live there for a year, during which time they definitely will appear to me. But money is the key. Money to purchase a car, secure the house, to buy food and necessities for a year, where to get this from? I have done some figuring and it would take about $5,000 to do what "they" want, in their way and time period.

Time No More

The Saucer Intelligence warn that time is growing short. That only they can stop our inexorable approach to a nuclear war with the resulting death of countless humans and the certainty of the United States being destroyed forever.

According to them we probably have only a year or two at maximum to avoid being destroyed. No time for years of "UFO investigation" by teams of scientists who can only get there after the UFOs are gone and perhaps discover, if you are lucky, that there really was a UFO there.

I have the immediate answer, not only for our government but for the entire world. But no takers it seems. It is utterly laughable. Millions or rather billions down the drain to kill in Vietnam, billions down the drain to foreign countries that hate us, billions down the drain to set up great society programs and I can't get the few thousand from them to meet with the SIs to save the U.S., then the world from themselves.

Proof Of Contacts

Now let me show you some proof of what I have been saying. For after all I wouldn't want you to accept anything just because you've read it here. You can check into the following for yourself and know that what I have said in the preceeding pages has been absolutely true, based upon actual contact with pilots of flying saucers.

On March 9, 1965, I wrote to George Clark, CIA, and others as follows:

"Nature* has told me to inform you that to prove it is using me as its representative, it will do something without my using PK, or knowing any of its workings. Nature will, in the near future, change the North and South Poles. As the message came to me, I believe it will use extreme heat to affect both those two places...and change the magnetic condition of the poles. Nature added that you won't have to check with any bureau on it...that the result will be strong enough to make the newspapers where you can read about it."

---

*At this time I thought Nature itself was in contact with me, not knowing it had anything to do with flying saucers.

On July 8, 1965, approximately four months later, the newspapers were filled with the account of a UFO which parked in the air over two scientific expeditions at the South Pole, allowed itself to be photographed and it changed the electromagnetic apparatus at the scientific bases there.

Also note that during my stay in Washington, D.C., while I was taking my message from the SIs to the government there was a tremendous appearance of UFOs in the Washington, D.C., and surrounding areas.

On July 21, 1965, I wrote to my government agencies and scientific contacts the following:

"The SIs state that they will begin an attack campaign on the United States with lightning. Lightning attacks everywhere. There will be an unusual abundance of lightning bolts striking everywhere, everything soon. Also my friends say that they will appear over one of our major U.S. cities soon, in one of their flying machines. They won't name the city, for security reasons -- theirs."

On July 31, 1965, the newspapers reported UFO sightings flooding not only this country but the world, most numerous sightings since 1957.

On August 4th, thousands of persons watched UFOs over Oklahoma City, across the nation's midlands and the Southwest. The article stated it was the fourth consecutive day of UFO sightings.

As for my lightning prediction here is the list of freak events which the SIs claim they caused:

July 30 three U.S. Marines in Vietnam were hit with a bolt of lightning.

August 9 two golfers in Louisville, Ga., were hit by bolts of lightning.

August 17 a bolt of lightning hit a stockpile of dynamite in Auburn, California, killing three men.

August 19 Albert Regeis of White Haven, Pa., was hit by a bolt of lightning on the beach.

August 19 a boy scout was hit by a bolt of lightning in Stokes State Forest, Branchville, New Jersey.

August 19 "Old Solo", one of the oldest and largest living things on the face of the earth, a giant redwood tree in Porterville, Cal., was struck by lightning in such a way the fire could not be put out.

But perhaps the most amazing freak lightning event happened on August 4th at Cape Kennedy. One man was killed and five injured when a bolt of lightning struck a rocket pad then under construction.

So you see when the Saucer Intelligence demonstrate, they demonstrate. And they call their shot beforehand, using a human -- me.

Need more proof? On August 6, 1965, I wrote to the usual contacts as follows:

"Now...I will let you in on something. Am calling fleets of UFOs here. To Philadelphia...from everywhere. Trouble is I do not know what they can do to prove to these people here that I'm for real...but I will think of something. Believe they are here already because I sent for them this afternoon. With all that power, whatever kind it is that they have...and it seems to be miraculous, judging from what they've accomplished this past year, they should do something startling. Am trying to convey the idea to them of coming right over the city and hovering. They give me the idea back that we might have some kind of rays like they have, or whatever it is they have, and hurt them or something. So that they are reticent to do this. So I am trying to tell them we haven't any such thing, and it's safe. I want to bring one down right over Market Street and have it hover there for 20 minutes. What else they'll do on their own is anybody's guess."

January 12, some five months later (evidently they waited so the government wouldn't set a trap) they appeared at the Wanaque Reservoir, near here, and were watched by police, the mayor, the Civil Defense director and countless people, as they stayed all night in the area, maneuvering with their craft...and they showed their ray! They shined it down onto the ice and the police and others who went to the spot found a large hole burned through the thick ice.

On April 19, 1966, I wrote my contaacts:

"When you read about the UFO seen in Philadelphia, in the days or weeks ahead... you will know who it is linking up with."

Only six days later, the famous "Fireball" flashed over the East Coast and over Philadelphia. Newsclippings have read "Flaming Meteor Seen Over Philadelphia" and it was written up in national magazines and debated upon whether it was a UFO or an actual meteor.

Why They Contacted Me

As I have gotten it from "them" rather spottily, they had worked with me since early childhood, attempting to get through to me. As I grew up, they kept trying. I worked for Dr.Rhine at Duke University in the ESP experimentation there and was found to be loaded with paranormal ability in the lab there. But the SIs still hadn't gotten through to me. It seems to have been a combination of the close approach of their UFO to our car in Fort Worth and then my work in the field of hypnosis in Fort Worth. Then my work in allied fields finally made it possible for them to get through to me.

    I might add at this point that years ago I did quite a bit of wandering myself over desert and mountain, even across Mexican desert where I am sure they must have contacted me. I recall now several instances when I was alone on a mountain top, or on a desert, under the stars wrapped in a blanket, when various "odd" things occured.

Odd Experiences

    You may be interested to know my wife and I have had a small circle of spinning vivid-colored light (many colours) in our apartment in Philadelphia. We woke up one night and there it was suspended overhead in our room. We were not dreaming. We watched it, fascinated, until it went away. Then she and I saw some strange things, separately, in our apartment. And just a few Mondays ago, at this writing, she went out onto the fire escape outside our windows for a breath of fresh air and something alive, about two feet long or high, dropped down from nowhere onto the fire escape not more than three feet from her and just crouched there. She dashed inside, scared to death. She saw it fall, heard the thump as it landed, and watched it for a split second as it crouched there, only moving slightly, then ran for dear life.

Also we have gotten what looks like long insect-like antennae on our TV screen many times. These twitching antennae move with life-like movements. Also some other odd things have appeared on there too. We are fairly certain this must be another way for the Saucer Intelligence to let us both know they are watching over us.

MESSAGE TO THE AMERICAN PEOPLE FROM THE FLYING SAUCER INTELLIGENCE

Sent through Ted H. Owens

We are happy that we are able to reach the ears of human beings after trying for long spaces of time. This human who is talking for us, we have been teaching for years in your time, and now he knows much and will know much more. He can do much. You must listen to him carefully and protect him for if you lose him you lose your link with us and it is not known for how long it may be until we find another human who can receive our thoughts and send intelligence back. It would be as if you were trying to teach your earth animals how to talk and suddenly you found one who could actually converse with you and through this one animal you had an opportunity to discover secrets of the animal kingdom. Through us you have the opportunity to discover the secrets of space, of far away places, of advanced technology, but better still you have the opportunity of surviving, for as a race you are utterly doomed now, as you are flying (this is their exact word). Many civilizations before you have so doomed themselves, and destroyed themselves, and we were helpless to give them assistance and advice and powerful aid. Now for the first time in long space ages we are able, through a human's senses, to come to the aid of a good civilization and help it to survive. But we can only do so if you listen and pay attention.

We are causing severe drought with our machines in your skies so that we can teach you a basic lesson which is that our intelligence is far superior to that of earth intelligence. We can control earth people because we can control what you call weather. When, and not before, our earth human has been accepted by your government and put to good use, then and only then will we release the drought conditions and let rainfall come in abundance down onto your thirsty earth. We will also add pestilance and sickness and what you call accidents; we will follow the structure of events which we used in the day of the human you know as Moses, as he strove against the ruler of the great country called Egypt. As we helped Moses in that day, so shall we help the human friend we know now as Ted Owens. It may please him to think that he is the "Rain Maker", of course, we make the rain for him, but what is the difference? So that you people of the earth will believe this message we send to you, and we do not expect you to believe it unless we show proof, listen carefully.

From now on, in time ahead, we will lift the drought for a little and let it rain where it is needed. Then, lest you think that it is a perchance, we will drop the curtain once more with our machines and let the rays of the sun penetrate the bowels of the earth and dry up your rivers, your lakes, your plants, until you accept our human as our representative.

After you accept him, we have much work for him to do, for we do not speak your language, nor do we know too much, as we should, about your inner workings. It is through this human that we can learn; and it is through us that you can learn.

Even now we send the meaning of our thoughts to him and his brain translates through pictures and feelings into your English. It is good.

Beware lest you take too long to accept our human friend, for then we must strike a hard blow at the country which spurns him, to punish your country as you would punish a child which persists in misbehaving. After your country has accepted our link and we are able to proceed in keeping earth humans from the time old habit of erasing themselves as civilizations, we will make your earth a wonderful place, the way it should be. We have no wish to rule you, or dictate you. We only wish, as friends, to know you and teach you and let you be happy. We are not flesh and blood such as you. Our composition is that of your grasshopper, so that our bodies will compress and expand with space work. We have no blood but different chemicals inside ourselves. We are small, but have the ability to reverse our body electricily at will and this gives us strength to move and to carry great burdens; makes us very strong. Language difficulty makes it difficult for us to send a stream of highly technical information through our human friend for translation, since he is not a scientist, and must therefore translate as he understands. But for a beginning it is good.

And may we ask you please be careful not to pursue our crafts in your curiosity, not to attack us with your weapons, simply because we are not like yourselves. When our human friend is in an area, please do not have planes overhead because you do not know it but we will have our craft

there as well. We have methods that make
our ship so that your earth eyes cannot
see them, at times. You ask if there is
anything else, earth friend. Just that we
are happy and excited for you and your
people and for us. Be patient and be careful for we cannot risk losing our human
friend-link. That is all.

ONE MAN 'SPACE INTELLIGENCE'

The Philadelphia Daily News
September 27, 1968

For awhile Ted Owens was content to cause rainstorms where there had been no rain for six years. He did work up that mystifying power blackout in 1967, when he snuffed out the light for the entire East Coast. Everybody grumbled about that, but nobody came clamoring after Owens with fistfulls of dollars to buy his cloud-bursting, light-snuffing services. That's when he turned to the Eagles.

"I had been to Washington," Owens explained the other day. "I had talked to NASA and the CIA. I tried to get them to use this power. They didn't understand it.

"I came up here and had spent all my money, I had to get a job. I started making rainstorms, writing in ahead. They only came when I said they would.

"In Washington I had controlled football games over TV. I'd bet on a game and wouldn't even take odds. I could take the Steelers to beat the Packers, with no odds. And the Steelers would beat the Packers.

"The SIs, that's Space Intelligence, urged me to get in touch with the Eagles. I wanted them to hire me as a special consultant. I would help them become champions. With the money they paid me I could go out to an isolated spot and arrange face-to-face contact with the SIs with top government figures."

The Eagles did just what any sane, healthy football organization would do.

They ignored Owens. Shazam. Dave Graham wrecked his ankle. Lane Howell ripped a knee, Mike Ditka injured leg; Gary Ballman, hamstring; Al Nelson, broken arm; Ron Medved, torn knee; Bob Brown, who had to be 9 to 5 over a grissly bear, out with a knee shredded by some ordinary human. Or was it?

"Sports is a superficial thing," Owens admitted, "but it's an excellent way to demonstrate the SIs power over a small group of men.

"I don't hear voices. Their communications with me come just as you'd get an idea for a column. Pow. I used to write them down. I don't have to now. It's a feeling like hearing a musical note. It's hard to describe. The woods are full of people who hear voices from outer space. So are the mental hospitals."

But Owens has a background in science and a hasty way of talking that is raspy with sincerity. And besides, look what has happened to the Eagles this season.

First off, Norm Snead broke his leg with nobody near him. Nobody the eye could see, anyway. Then all those guys got hurt against Miami, an AFL team that's fluffier than popcorn. Then 24 guys got sick before the Green Bay game. And in every instance, Owens had written a letter the week of the game forecasting the disaster. The scientist would scoff. Pure coincidence. On any given Sunday, any given number of guys are going to get hurt.

"I'm working with a medium I never worked with in my life," he said. "I can ask them to bring about certain results. Before the Miami game I might ask them to get as many players out of action and they knocked out eight.

"I had the feeling early Sunday that they were gonna win that game. I knew the PK had to be hiked up. I contacted the SIs and told them the problem. They said they would send a UFO over the field and control the game."

Written by Stan Hochman

Any readers wishing to write the author may do so at the following address:

> Ted Owens
> Box 48
> Cape Charles, Va. 23310

Ted Owens, author of HOW TO CONTACT SPACE PEOPLE claims to have predicted east coast black-out with help of space people.

www.ingramcontent.com/pod-product-compliance
Lightning Source LLC
Chambersburg PA
CBHW051714090426
42736CB00013B/2695